For
p...
enjoy!
♡rachel

Recipoetry
of a
Kitchen Mystic

by Rachel Ballantine

A Cookbook Scrapbook
of
Original Recipes, Poetry, Art
2012
Word Girl Press

For you to enjoy.
Love, Rachel ♡

Rachel Ballantine

This book is
dedicated to
All of The Ancestors

Thank You — ♡

Table of Contents

Table of Contents

Dear Reader,

In the olden days, the most important books -- and sometimes the only books -- a woman had were her Bible and her cookbook.

Her cookbook was usually a collection of recipes, a record of events, words of inspiration and comfort, how to take care of home, how to heal, and how to cook.

This book honors all the ancestors: the grandmothers, the mothers, the aunties, the sisters, the neighbors -- all of whom embody the feminine.

It is created to look like the old cookbook-scrapbooks of the women who have gone before.

I honor their lives.

Since the beginning, women have been the cooks and the keepers of the hearth and I believe we need to remember and connect to them. We are all related through cooking and food.

It is my hope that the poems, collages and recipes will nurture body and soul and create connection between women across time and cultures, and be of comfort and inspiration.

Much deliciousness to you!

Love,

Rachel

Apple Salad

Dressing;

    2 eggs, beaten very light

    ½ cup butter

    1½ cups sugar

    2 tbls vinegar

Boil 20 minutes stirring allthe time

at first to keep from lumping.

    Thin with sweet cream.

    Chop apples and add English Walnut

meats or any soft nuts.

COOKED SALAD DRESSING
(1½ cups)

1 teaspoon salt
1 teaspoon dry mustard
  Few grains cayenne pepper
2 tablespoons flour
2 tablespoons sugar or light
  corn sirup
2 egg yolks or 1 egg
1 cup evaporated milk
¼ cup vinegar or lemon juice

Blend salt, mustard, cayenne, flour, and sugar. Add egg yolks, mix well, and add milk. Cook over boiling water until the mixture thickens, stirring constantly. Cool. Stir in vinegar or lemon juice slowly. A few drops of onion juice may be added. If you wish to use this dressing with fresh fruit, combine it with an equal amount of whipped cream.

making a salad every day
is an act of prayer.
My mother is a salad genius.
With some leaves, some oil,
some garlic, she makes a salad
that is greater than the sum
of its parts.
In the early 1950's, my father
carved a big wooden salad bowl.
Then my mother mashed garlic in it
creating a patina, an atmosphere
for salad. One time, I figured out
how many salads she'd made in
the big wooden bowl.
I called her up.
Mom, I said, you've made over
seventeen thousand salads!
Thank you sweetheart, she said.
Thank you for adding that up
for me.
      RB

One Dollar Award.
Mrs. George Hughes, 119 Second
street, N. W., Mason City.
(Hallowe'en Menu)
Frankfurters in Finger Rolls
Spook Salad
Brown Bread and Butter
Sandwiches
Pennsylvania Pumpkin Pie
Coffee

Spook Salad.

One head lettuce.
One cup chopped celery.
One cup diced apples.
One cup red grapes, seeded and halved.
Six halves of peaches.
Mayonnaise.

  Blend the celery, apples, grapes with mayonnaise make a nest of shredded lettuce on each plate. Put a portion of the salad on each one. On this salad place a half peach with the rounded side up. Insert two whole cloves for the eyes, place another with the large end down for the nose and a narrow strip of pimento for the mouth.

6

When Women Invented Writing

When women invented writing
it was so they could share recipes
recipes are the most important thing
in the world because it is, after all,
through olives and sunlight
that spirit becomes flesh
recipes are the alchemy of the goddess
the maps of how to transform the greens
and grains of the great goddess into
the sacred delicious sustenance of life

Here is how to ferment grapes,
this is how to let the bread rise,
now is when to add salt,
here is how to knead, to stir, to dry,
to add oil, to make yogurt,
what to feed the baby when her tummy hurts.

Add rose petals to rice and you will know love,
cook in your iron skillet because the iron in our blood
comes from the stars and our blood needs that,
needs salt from the sea, our hearts need rose petals,
our bones need greens, our feet need sesame oil,
and our thoughts need fragrance and butter.

Barley becomes hope and mint teaches delight
almonds keep secrets and cardamom is full of mystery

Think of your flesh and your dreams!
It is through water and love
we are created.
It is time now
to wake up from the bitter dream,
and it is time now
to make our lives sweet.

by rachel

But now to come to my story. It was a dull day in December, the week before Christmas, when Mr. Cowan entered a comfortable drawing-room where a party of ladies and a little girl were sitting

R3, Clinton, Wis., June 15, 1953

In 1952 I harvested 80 bus. corn to the acre on 30 acres corn fertilized with Royster's 3-12-12-18-7-1, 200 lbs. per acre. Royster's is a fine fertilizer. I've been using it for 10 years, and during that time have never had a bag to give me trouble—it doesn't get lumpy and is much easier to handle than other makes.
OGDEN INMAN

16ª Monday. Lunedì

Oggi primo giorno di lavoro della settimana. Mi alzo presto alle cinque e mezzo po preparo per la colazione e lavo i piatti che cueste il lavoro di tutti i giorni. Poi comincio lavare e stirare sempre con le machine la servo i piatti e à dormire

Why Better Flavoring makes Better Cooks

1930 SCHOOL
Wouldn't you enjoy spending two weeks with this group of Hoosier girls and join them in the study of all the phases of better home-making?

HOTEL TURAN
«BEST HOTEL İN KAYSERİ»
RESTAURANT AND PASTRY SHOP

MUSTAFA AND AHMET TURAN

WITH TOİLET, HOT AND COLD WATER AND SHOWERS IN EVERY ROOMS. TURKİSH BATHS AND LİFT.
FOR HOME COMFORD TRY HOTEL TURAN
RESSERVATİONS CAN BE MADE İN ADVANCE

ALL SIGHT-SEEING TOURS CAN BE ARRENGED BY OUR GUİDES.

CABLE
HOTEL TURAN

ADDRESS

PHONE
1968

2

Muffins.

3 c Flour
4 ts Baking Powder
4 tb sugar
4 tb shortening or fat
½ to salt
2 eggs
Liquid to make a drop batter
Sift the dry materials together
Add the beaten egg and liquid
Then melted fat. Beat thorough
Then put in greased muffin
pans. Bake in hot oven

Vivan's Angle Food Cake

1¼ c. sugar —
1 cup Swans Down —
½ to salt — 1 to Cream o Tartar
1 to Vanilla — ½ to Almond —
1 cup Egg whites —
Add salt to Egg Whites & beat until
frothy — then sift cream o Tartar
over top — fold in 1 cup sugar
2 tbl at a time —
Sift ¼ c sugar with the flour
4 times — Then fold into
the egg whites —
Put in ungreased tube pan
& bake one hour at 375°

Which Fork Would *You* Have Used—
or would you have used a spoon?

Devils Food Cake(cocoa)

½C butter
1 teas vanilla
¼ teas salt
1&3/4C sugar
½Ccocoa
1C water(cold)
2C siftedcake flour
1 teas soda
1 tbls hot water
3 egg whites

Cream butter, salt & vanilla. Add sugar
gradually then cocoa and 2 tbls cold water.
When well creamed add flour and remaining
C. water in 4 additions, beating between each
Next add soda dissolved in warmwater, then be
beatenegg whites.   Bake as layers or loaf in
a moderate oven(350 f) until cake shrinks fro
sides of pan about 25 min for layer & 45 for
loaf.

Jesus Bread

Mix $\frac{1}{4}$ cup oil

1$\frac{1}{4}$ cups water

$\frac{1}{2}$ tsp salt

Mix in about 3 cups of whole wheat flour and $\frac{1}{2}$ cup
of whole amaranth to make a stiff dough.
Knead until smooth.
Put in nice big bowl, cover with a clean cloth and
leave for 24 hours.
Soak 2 cups spelt or whole wheat kernels during the
same 24 hours in 2 cups of water.
Drain the grains and chop in blender.
Knead the grains into the dough, a little at a time.
Make 2 round loaves.
Set on a baking sheet;
Let rise 20 minutes.
Bake about one to one and a half hours at 325 degrees.

Serve with sweet dark red wine and really good cheese
and a dish of olives and maybe some dried herring.

by Rachel

Grace—Mrs Dyson is having another "Mad Tantrum." She asked for a sleeping pill so I gave her two of Pope's white one's & told her to take one at 7:PM and if she wasn't asleep at 11: to take the other one. She flew up as usual & said it wouldn't do any good to take it before 11: meaning there was to much noise & talking up untill that time. So I took the tablets away & told her I would leave them for you to give her.

So give her one of Popes Phenobarbs. at 7:PM if she will take it. & another at 11: if needed.

ViRA.

Some Excellent Relishes

Chili Sauce—Use firm, rather underripe tomatoes for this. Cut one in small pieces and place in the bottom of the can. Add several slices of green or red sweet peppers, and a layer of sliced white onion. Place tomato over this, and more onion and peppers. A few pieces of pared ripe cucumber, which has been soaked in boiling water for a few minutes, may be mixed with the onion, if liked, and the small yellow or red cherry tomatoes may be used instead of large ones. They are not freed from skins in that case. Place a heaping teaspoon salt in the top of each quart can, with a small pinch ceyenne pepper and a little white pepper, if liked. Leave space enough in the can for half cup vinegar to each quart can. Process one hour. (See Farm and Home Cook Book.)—[L. W. M., No A 378, F W H L.

Sweet Cucumber Pickle—Put cucumbers in cold, weak brine (1½ cups salt to one gallon water) one day and night. Take out, dry on cloth. To one gallon vinegar add two cups sugar, and nearly one ounce mixed spice. Heat these all boiling hot. Put the pickles into this and let boil up once. Put into sterilized cans immediately and pour the hot vinegar over them, then seal. They are excellent, are nice and sweet, and will not shrivel, if you follow directions. One gallon vinegar will cover two gallons cucumbers.—[Mrs Emma Standing, No A 551, F W H L.

Mustard Pickle—Prepare one pint each lima beans, small onions, cauliflower, sweet pickles, celery, green tomatoes, and carrots, also three sweet green peppers and three sweet red peppers. Measure out 1¾ pounds sugar, one-third cup flour, three tablespoons mustard, quarter tablespoon tumeric and one quart vinegar. Boil beans, carrots and onions in salt water until tender. Put tomatoes, celery, peppers and cauliflower in brine over night. Drain well in morning. Mix flour, tumeric and mustard together with cold vinegar, and cook thick and creamy, then mix all together, and cook 10 minutes. Seal —[Mrs E. S. Brown

Rudwingeb an Leon Albin

12

Slightly Green Spread
for toast or crackers
by rachel

One and a half cups toasted
pumpkin seeds
Three hard boiled eggs
Juice of two lemons
Hunk a blue cheese (about ½ cup)
Capers (about ¼ cup)
Salt
1/3 block cream cheese
1/2 cup half and half

Blend in Blender

This will make your brain
very happy! ♡

Kiwi

The way Lois ate the kiwi
was a ceremony of clean lines.
In the kitchen she got a cutting board
and a clean shiny sharp knife.
She placed them in front
of her crossed legs on the floor
and sliced through the fuzzy brown
kiwi, exposing its wet and green black
secrets.
Her clean white even teeth bit into
the clean green kiwi.
She ate its tart secrets with great dignity
and careful delight, and then
smacked her lips and grinned.
On the cutting board were ther
carefully sliced slices of fuzzy kiwi rind.
In astonishment I knew that was the most
well eaten kiwi
I would ever witness

by rachel

THE MAD BULL.   3

Then there is another thing which I
hope you do not forget to do. And that
is, to put yourselves into God's hand, under his keeping, and ask him to take care
of you through the coming day. You
little know what dangers may be near
you over and over again through the day.
And as it is only God who can keep you
from harm, you should remember always
to ask him to do so. I knew a little boy

Rules for Making Frostings

Follow These 5 Rules

1. Use one part boiling water to three parts sugar.
2. Cover the saucepan and let the syrup boil three or four minutes; the steam will melt any grains of sugar remaining on the sides of the dish.
3. Let boil undisturbed until the syrup reach-es the soft-ball stage.
4. Pour in a fine stream on the egg-white, beaten very light, beating constantly.
5. Beat occasionally until cold.

Test for Sugar Cooked to Soft Ball

In making most cooked frostings for cake, sugar with water enough to dissolve it is cooked to the soft-ball degree, or from 236 degrees to 242 degrees F. Without a ther-mometer, test the syrup by dropping a little of it into cold water, and if it may be gathered together into a soft ball (in the water), or if when the the syrup drops from the spoon, a hair-like thread, two or three inches in length appears, the right degree is reached.

Test for Sugar Cooked to Hard Ball

When the cooking of the sugar and water is continued to about 248 degrees F., the hard-ball degree is reached; at this degree a little of the syrup may be gathered together in a little cold water to form a hard ball.

MILLINERY

MRS. A. F. ASHLEY

HEMSTITCHING - PICOTING

DRESSES, APRONS, TABLE SCARFS, PILLOW CASES
AND FANCY WORK

PHONE 324

Bon Bon Cookies

Mix thoroughly
½ cup soft butter
¾ " sifted confectioners
                          sugar
1 tbsp. vanilla

Mix in by hand
1½ cups sifted flour
⅛ tsp. salt
(If to dry add 1-2 tbsp.
cream as needed.)

Press dough around center
such as date, gumdrop, cherry,
nuts, chocolate square, coconut
or what you may dream up.

Bake on ungreased sheet
350° 12-15 min. just till
set, not brown
Dip in icing while warm

14

Butter Pecan Chocolate Chip Cookies
by Rachel

Cream together:
  1 cup butter
  1/3 cup sugar
Add: One egg
  1 tsp vanilla
  1/2 tsp salt
  1/4 tsp grated orange rind
  dash nutmeg
  1/4 cup chocolate chips
  1/4 cup pecans

  1 cup mixed together
      flour, ground flaxseed
      and wheat germ

Roll into balls
Smush with palm.
Bake 10-12 minutes
  on greased cookie sheet
♡

4022

CARE OF PRESSURE COOKER

Cleanliness is the first rule in the care of a pressure cooker. At each washing look to see that vent tube is clear — a pipe cleaner is a help in cleaning it. Covers with pressure gages should never be immersed in water, nor should the weights that are used to control pressure. It is usually best not to put any type of cover in the dishpan because bits of food or grease might find their way to the vent tube.

Wash the gasket well; the rubber or rubberlike compound may be injured if grease accumulates on it. Some gaskets are removable for thorough washing.

Avoid damage to the rims of cooker and lid. These are the sealing surfaces and a dent could cause a leak that would make it difficult or impossible to build up steam pressure.

Do not cover the cooker tightly when it is not in use. Leave the cover loose so that air can circulate. Have a special place for the detachable weight and always put it there—otherwise you may lose as much time hunting it as you save by using the pressure pan.

Homemade Applesauce

4 pounds apple
¼ cup water
1 cup sugar

Wash apples. Without pelling or coring cut into quarters and cut away bad spots. Place apples into large sauce pan. Add water and cook covere 15 to 20 minutes until soft, stirring occasional. Spoon apples a third at a time into food chopper and strain thru mill. Add sugar & stir to dissol If applesauce is too juicy, return to food mill & let water drain off. Makes 6 cups or enough for applesauce cake and left overs.

It is fall and I want to
write you a poem.

What shall I tell you?
How the four light and dark
green zuchinnis are getting along
with the green dishes on
the counter?

How the garden is not yearning
for the sun but now
yearning for the earth?

How sad I am that I do not
have a fireplace to
gather wood for?

It seems fall is a time of gathering;
berries, wood, a pulling in.

Shall I tell you that the pinto beans
cooking smell so good with the incense,
and that Fluffy is looking like she's
ready for winter.
She has her snowsuit on.

by rachel °l°9

17

DAY DREAMS, VISIONS OF BLISS

WERBA & LUESCHER'S PRODUCTION OF THE VIENNESE OPERETTA

THE SPRING MAID

MIZZI H

Two Kinds of Women.

When one says, "She is a woman of the world," the phrase does not imply in the least that she is a worldly woman. Such an one enjoys only those delights that are essentially of the earth earthy. Pleasure is her aim and fashion her god; but a "woman of the world" is an entirely different type altogether. She is, to give a concise definition, one who possesses a rare knowledge of the world, gained by a wide and varied personal experience. A woman of the world is wise, and can sit in judgment on men and affairs, because she knows whereof she speaks, while a worldly woman in many cases hasn't a single sensible idea in her frivolous head. A woman of the world is to be trusted. She is, as a rule, cool and calculating, with a discrimination worthy of a diplomat. She never reveals the secret of another or tells any of her own. She does more thinking than talking, but what she says always means something. She rarely condemns, for from her vast experience she knows that there is good in everyone, and that the motive for many a seemingly ill-advised action may be of the purest, though the thing itself seems grossly unconventional. The worldly woman, on the other hand, looks no deeper than the surface, and is influenced entirely by what society would say.

Day Dreams, Visions of Bliss
Duet: Bozena and Aladar

erato con moto

Reinhardt

The First Woman

When the first fish-woman
walked out of the sea, she
made a little fire to dry off,
then she gathered some leaves
and made a cup of tea.
She wove herself a light shawl
and searched for some pretty
shells to make some earrings.
Sometime later, say, a few thousand
millenia, fish-man crawled out of
the sea. It took him several
thousand years but he grew legs,
learned to climb, then walk upright,
and finally, he discovered fire!
The fire he discovered was the woman's
cooking fire. She had some bread baking
from the wheat she had grown; a fine
dish of yogurt from her pet sheep's
milk, and she was writing a poem
with a dip pen and sepia ink.
He was naked, and late
for supper.

by rachel ♡

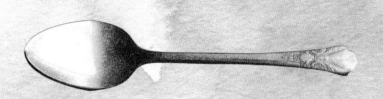

My Ideal Garden
by Rachel

I will grow big fancy words that come out
in calligraphy and some antique gold lacy
dishes. My garden has a fountain in each corner
of lapis and jade and I will grow gemstones
and pearls and special treats for Fluffy.
I will grow a boyfriend that doesn't lie
and I will grow lots of paper and an earring tree
is just outside the window.
Over in the corner is a nice little shoe bush with
mules with tufts of bunny fur and sneakers that
light up and glossy red high heels.
I will have a nicely cultivated row of ancient
manuscripts, perhaps a patch of pots and pans
and a short row of red nail polish.
My garden has a year round growing season and there
aren't many weeds.
If I need some ravioli I'll just go to the kitchen
plot and pick a little for supper.
Maybe I will have some spices and exotic jars
of fruit already canned just waiting to be picked.
And oh, yes, the money tree with gold coins, enough
for everybody to come and pick.
I am such a good gardener!
I can have a little roadside stand and sell
poems in a jar.
Anything anybody needs, I will go find it in my
garden, looking under bushes or up in the tree,
and it will be there.

HOW TO MAKE SYRUP

Any fruit may be successfully canned in a syrup of any density. The sweetness desired in the finished product should govern the syrup used.

No. 1 Thin Syrup—Use three parts of water or fruit juice to one part of sugar and bring to a boil.

No. 2 Medium Syrup—Use two parts water or fruit juice to one part of sugar and bring to a boil.

No. 3 Heavy Syrup—Use one part of water or fruit juice to one part of sugar and bring to a boil.

The **Thin** syrups are generally used for small, soft fruits, as sweet cherries, berries, etc.

Medium syrups are generally used on peaches, sour berries, acid fruits, as rhubarb, cherries, gooseberries, etc.

Heavy syrups are generally used on larger sour fruits that are to be extra sweet.

18

21

17   caro   100

19   scarpe gelato   300
    gelato e manzo   20
    caro   27
18   candelle e gelato   75
    Marro
    candele   50
  petone irene palone erna   20
  cravate   30
  i braciaceti   20
  dolci   40
  dolci   30
  ruotole   20
  carro   30
20 per   10
21 in ch
venerdi co
per move.

Would you eat soup this way?

Always drink bouillon— never eat it with a spoon

The napkin should not be used like a towel—

Is this the correct way to hold the fork?

Should a Man Put on a Woman's Rubbers?

Soft Molasses Cookies

3 cups flour (sifted); 1½ teaspoons baking powder; ¼ teaspoon soda; ½ teaspoon ginger; 1½ teaspoons cinnamon; ½ cup melted shortening; 1 cup molasses; 2 tablespoons warm water; 1 egg, beaten.

Tangy Deviled Eggs

Cut in half lengthwise 6 hard-boiled eggs. Mash the yolks and blend in ¼ cup mayonnaise, 1 tablespoon grated horse radish, 1 tablespoon chopped dill pickle, 1 tablespoon chopped parsley, ½ teaspoon salt, ¼ teaspoon dry mustard and ⅛ teaspoon paprika. Fill egg halves with mixture and serve.

Sweet Potato Biscuits

First, sift together 1 cup flour, 3 teaspoons baking powder and ½ teaspoon salt, and then add 4 tablespoons fat and a cup of cooked, mashed sweet potatoes. Now add ½ to ¾ cup milk to make stiff enough to roll, cut and bake in hot oven 20 to 30 minutes.

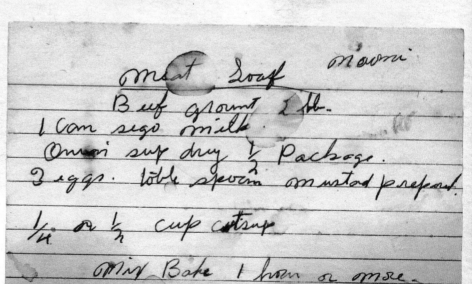

Meat Loaf   mami
Beef ground 2 lb.
1 can sego milk
Onion sup dry ½ Package.
3 eggs. table spoon mustard prepard
¼ or ½ cup catsup
Mix Bake 1 hour or more.

IS in Town
Room 412 At Bonc
call her if you
want to go
get a sangwhich

Leanna's Strawberry Preserves.

Take Equal parts by weight of
strawberries and sugar. Take ½ the sugar and
add a little water and boil until it spins
a thread, then add the rest of the berries
and sugar. Boil from 7 to 10 min. Seal.

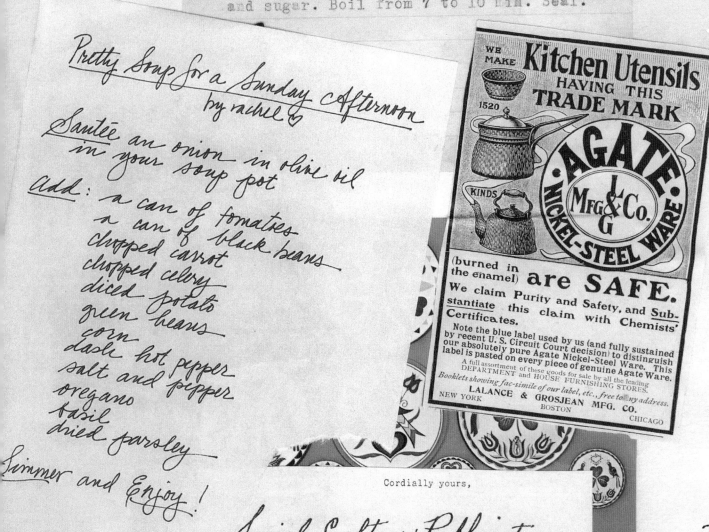

Pretty Soup for a Sunday Afternoon
by rachel ♡

Sautée an onion in olive oil
in your soup pot
Add: a can of tomatoes
a can of black beans
chopped carrot
chopped celery
diced potato
green beans
corn
dash hot pepper
salt and pepper
oregano
basil
dried parsley

Simmer and Enjoy!

Cordially yours,

Social Culture Publications

23

IT DOESN'T MATTER WHAT THEY THINK

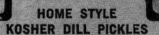

— MOM

Surf Pot Stew
by rachel ♡

Sautée: one Italian sausage
cut up

1/2 large onion chopped

4 oz chicken

Add: 1 can clams

1/4 cup red wine

1 can white beans

chopped celery

cayenne

salt & pepper

water or broth

Simmer ~

HOME STYLE
KOSHER DILL PICKLES

To each quart jar add:
1 head fresh dill
2 to 3 cloves garlic
(depending on size)
1 small red or green hot
pepper (optional)

Select fresh-firm cucumbers—
wash and pack in jars
Bring to a boil:
2 quarts water
1 quart Speas distilled or
cider vinegar
1 cup non-iodized salt

Pour hot solution over cucumbers and seal. Pickles will be ready in 3 to 4 weeks depending on the size of the cucumbers. For plain dill pickles the garlic buds can be omitted.

OUR 75th YEAR

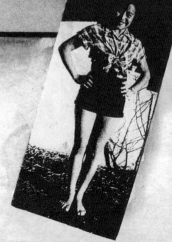

Soup Song
by rachel ♡

Every soup you make has a song,
   a sound, a note — a chord.
It will vibrate with the feeling
you had as you made it.

Be Conscious when cooking.

Do not eat food made by angry
   or drunk people.

Cook with absolute respect in your heart.
Cook with patience, and appreciation.
Make a soup that is a chorus.
Maybe it will be a one or two note
   delicate melody.
For example, a light egg drop soup.
Or it may be a symphony stew.
Or a humming vegetable soup.
Or a rowdy bean soup.
Cook the song songs — eating them
makes music in your blood.

25

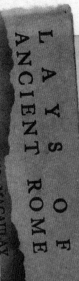
A

THOUSAND WAYS

TO PLEASE A HUSBAND

WITH
BETTINA'S BEST RECIPES

—BY—

LOUISE BENNETT WEAVER
AND
HELEN COWLES LeCRON

The Romance of Cookery
AND HOUSEKEEPING

Puts on her silken vestments white,
And tricks her hair in lovely plight

Early Barbarian Stew
(700 BC)

Channelled by Rachel Ballantine.

Chuck Roast	Cut the roast
Carrots	into large cubes,
Onions	put into an iron
Potatoes	skillet with oil.
Dried Figs	Add cubes of beets,
Dried Cranberries	onions, potatoes,
Dates	diced dates, figs,
Sundried Tomatoes	tomatoes.
Salt	Sprinkle with salt,
Pepper	pepper, cayenne, garlic,
Cayenne Pepper	and crushed dried
Beets	herbs.
Garlic	Add about 1/4" of
Sherry	sherry and put
Oil	in the oven on
Dried Mint	350° for about
Dried Parsley	an hour.
Dried Tarragon	

RB

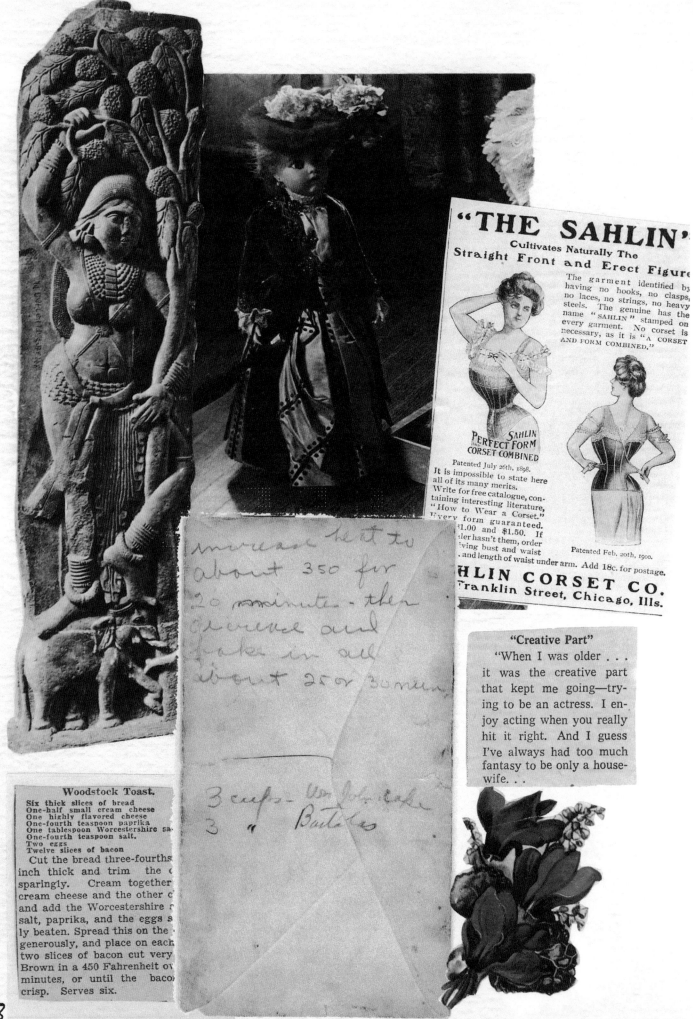

"THE SAHLIN"
Cultivates Naturally The
Straight Front and Erect Figure

The garment identified by having no hooks, no clasps, no laces, no strings, no heavy steels. The genuine has the name "SAHLIN" stamped on every garment. No corset is necessary, as it is "A CORSET AND FORM COMBINED."

SAHLIN
PERFECT FORM
AND
CORSET COMBINED

Patented July 26th, 1898.
It is impossible to state here all of its many merits. Write for free catalogue, containing interesting literature, "How to Wear a Corset." Every form guaranteed. $1.00 and $1.50. If ...ler hasn't them, order ...ving bust and waist ...and length of waist under arm. Add 18c. for postage.

Patented Feb. 20th, 1900.

...HLIN CORSET CO.
...Franklin Street, Chicago, Ills.

increase heat to about 350 for 20 minutes - then ... and bake in all about 25 or 30 min.

3 cups ... John cake
3 " Butter

"Creative Part"

"When I was older . . . it was the creative part that kept me going—trying to be an actress. I enjoy acting when you really hit it right. And I guess I've always had too much fantasy to be only a house-wife. . .

Woodstock Toast.
Six thick slices of bread
One-half small cream cheese
One highly flavored cheese
One-fourth teaspoon paprika
One tablespoon Worcestershire sa...
One-fourth teaspoon salt.
Two eggs
Twelve slices of bacon

Cut the bread three-fourths ... inch thick and trim the ... sparingly. Cream together ... cream cheese and the other c... and add the Worcestershire ... salt, paprika, and the eggs s... ly beaten. Spread this on the ... generously, and place on each ... two slices of bacon cut very ... Brown in a 450 Fahrenheit ov... minutes, or until the baco... crisp. Serves six.

28

Tomorrow I Will Give You

Tomorrow I will give you
    A bright green fruit
    One made of plaster
to gnaw on in your frustration
        (its taste is chalk)
        (its scent is white)
You can put it in the center
        of a large bowl
        on a long table
and the disciples will know
it was you, and your frustration
        by the shape
        of your teeth marks.

Tomorrow I will give you
    a jar of olive oil
brought from Rome
as sweet as the day it was made
        (its color is ancient)
        (its taste is divine)
    You can dip pieces
      of the green plaster fruit
    in this oil
    to make it edible
to nourish you through your journey
    of walking on stones

Tomorrow I will give you
    a pair of sandals
    of thin hammered gold
        (their scent is freedom)
        (their sound is holy)

by rachel

29

Tuna Casserole

3 tbls chopped green pepper
1/3tbls fat

1 teas salt
6 tbls flour

1 10 1/2 oz can condensed chicken
soup

1 1/2 cups milk

1 7oz can Tuna fish

1 tbls lemon juice

Brown onion and pepper in hot fat
  add salt and flour: blend.
Add chicken soup and milk; cook until
  sauce is thick and smooth

  Add tuna fish, flaked and the lemon juice

  Pour into greased baking dish and cover wit

tiny bisquits. Bake in ahot oven for 15 min

and then reduce to 425 for 15 min.

Serves 6

Plain Talks on Avoided Subjects
The Mystery of Sex Revealed in Plain English

The secret questions and thoughts of thousands answered in understandable language. This book is solemnly dedicated to set forth in clear language the conception and birth of a child; to follow the life of the male and the female from birth to maturity, explaining the function of love, sexual desire and passions; to advise those whose passions and sexual desires are stronger than their will to resist; to point out the demoralizing effects of self-abuse as practiced by both sexes; to instruct the bride who is ignorant of sexual knowledge and of the desires of the male which must be satisfied in order to perpetuate harmony in wedlock; to explain the evil effects of birth control as practiced by many women; to give advice to the unfortunate.

Making a Poached Egg

I broke an egg into
a shallow pan of boiling water
which at first greatly excited
the water bubbles, they tried
to engulf it

the thin egg white spread out
and became
misty like a gathering
fog over Chinese mountains
and then there was a ring
around a hot yellow moon

then the moon waned into
a frosty pale yellow
like it was in an eclipse
and then the water bubbles
completely covered it all with
an opaque froth, like waves
crashing
upon a rock.

I could not see the egg,
I waited, watching,
then I dipped it out with a
slotted spoon

it had gathered unto itself
glossy, smooth, coagulated
quivering and quite
tasty

by rachel

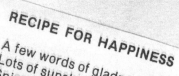

RECIPE FOR HAPPINESS

MIX-- A few words of gladness, with
Lots of sunshine
Spiced with a bit of humor
Sift out all unkindness.

ADD-- Good deeds as needed
Combine all and use daily.

Bavarian Cream.

½ PK. Geletine in ½ cup cold
water.
1 Pt Pine Apple. 1 cup sugar
Juice one lemon.
1 Pt cream; whipp cream real stiff
heat sugar pine apple and juice
of one lemon and pour over
Geletine let stand till cold and
beat, then beat cream and
all together.

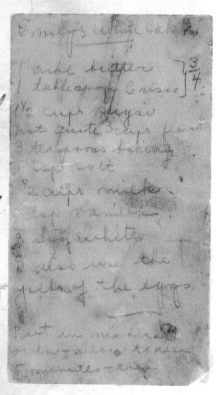

FUN IN THE KITCHEN

The only fun I ever had
In cake or candy making,
Was when I had a child to lick
The dishes used in baking.

32

Happy Peasant Soup
<u>   </u>

Sautee: 3 thick smoky slices bacon
              (cut up)
           1 large onion (diced)
           2 (cut up) chicken apple
               sausages

 water in soup pot
 add: the onion and meat
      1/2 parsnip diced
      2 potatoes diced
      3 stalks celery diced
      2 carrots diced
      1/2 cup dried nettles
      1/2 small acorn squash
          (peeled and diced)
        handful dried or fresh
            parsley
      1 cup black beans
      1 cup baby lima beans
      1 cup fresh green beans
      garlic powder, cayenne powder,
  salt and pepper
            simmer
                  by rachel

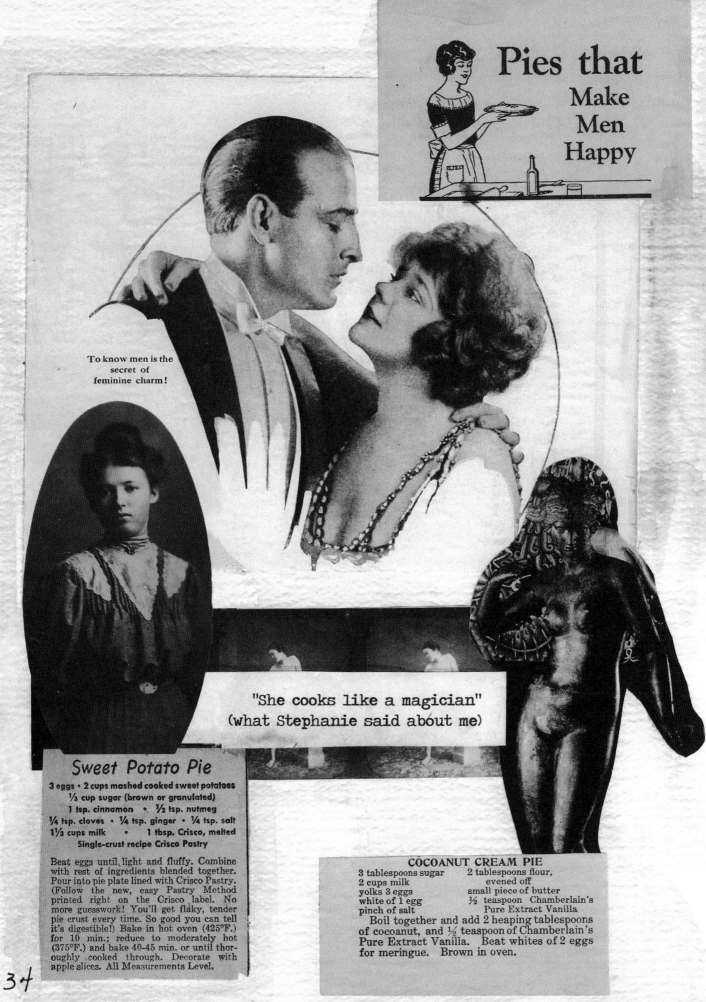

Pies that Make Men Happy

To know men is the secret of feminine charm!

"She cooks like a magician"
(what Stephanie said about me)

Sweet Potato Pie

3 eggs • 2 cups mashed cooked sweet potatoes
⅓ cup sugar (brown or granulated)
1 tsp. cinnamon • ½ tsp. nutmeg
¼ tsp. cloves • ¼ tsp. ginger • ¼ tsp. salt
1⅓ cups milk • 1 tbsp. Crisco, melted
Single-crust recipe Crisco Pastry

Beat eggs until light and fluffy. Combine with rest of ingredients blended together. Pour into pie plate lined with Crisco Pastry. (Follow the new, easy Pastry Method printed right on the Crisco label. No more guesswork! You'll get flaky, tender pie crust every time. So good you can tell it's digestible!) Bake in hot oven (425°F.) for 10 min.; reduce to moderately hot (375°F.) and bake 40-45 min. or until thoroughly cooked through. Decorate with apple slices. All Measurements Level.

COCOANUT CREAM PIE

3 tablespoons sugar   2 tablespoons flour,
2 cups milk   evened off
yolks 3 eggs   small piece of butter
white of 1 egg   ½ teaspoon Chamberlain's
pinch of salt   Pure Extract Vanilla

Boil together and add 2 heaping tablespoons of cocoanut, and ½ teaspoon of Chamberlain's Pure Extract Vanilla. Beat whites of 2 eggs for meringue. Brown in oven.

34

Cutting the orange required
the monk's total attention.

 The orange was the same
color as his robe.
 As he sliced into the skin
the oils fanned out, scenting
his hands and the wind chimes tinkled,
oblivious to this act.

He felt as if he were cutting
into the world, this world orange,
this holy man a planet sectioner.

He laid the succulent pieces
like a flower onto a black plate
and brought it as an offering to lay
among candles and baskets of rice
and the orange looked sweetly,
hopefully alive, vibrant,
with the spicy oily scent
of its own sacrifice
its being an offering to the gods

and they were pleased.

The monk turned away,
 his robe softly swishing
his legs.

by rachel

35

Foolproof Dumplings.

One egg beaten light.
One tablespoon sour milk.
Three-fourths cup flour.
One and one-fourth teaspoons baking powder.
One-fourth teaspoon salt.
Mix dry ingredients together, then add wet ingredients slowly while stirring. Drop by spoonfuls into boiling broth and cook 20 minutes.

S. Hohenshelt,   Artist.

The Food Doctor

Now that cucumbers are moderately priced, serve them as salad instead of in salad. Peel, cut into lengthwise quarters, place on salad greens and top with this terrific dressing: ½ pound crumbled blue cheese, 1 cup mayonnaise, ½ cup soured cream, juice of ½ lemon and a little grated onion. Mix or whip ingredients and store in refrigerator jars. This is good, too, on lettuce wedges and tomato slices. And it is elegant as spread for rye bread or dip for chips. Thin with a bit of milk to make dip.

A Woman's Sensitive Fingers.

Miss Calhoun, one of the most expert money-handlers in the treasury department at Washington, has the remarkable record of counting 85,000 coins in a single day, each coin passing through her hands; and so delicate has her sense of touch become that should there be a counterfeit coin in the lot she would detect it, even when counting at that tremendous rate. She spreads the coins upon a large glass-top desk, and draws them off with the tips of her fingers, one, two, three or four at a time, as she pleases, for her four fingers are all equally educated to the work. Her eyes have nothing to do with the detection of false coins. Her fingers do it all. They have become so very familiar with the exact weight of a true coin, the feeling of it, and the amount of its resistance upon the glass desk, that a piece of spurious gold, silver, nickel or copper money attracts her attention instantly.

POSTA

October, 1897, has 31 days.

The Henpecked Husband.

The woman that henpecks her husband am berry numerous in dis heah kermunity.

De American gal takes naturally ter henpeckin' her husband as soon as she has got one. Befoah she am married she thinks for herself. After she is married she thinks for him, too.

Bredderen and sistern, ter my mind one of de most solemnous fac's am dat Benjermen Franklin neber discobered de lightnin' ontil after he was done married. Hit's de same wid lots ob men whose names hain't Franklin. I can prove dat by you, can't I Uncle Mose?

I nebber knowed ob but one man who boasted dat he had nebber given his wife a cross word in twenty years, and de nobors allowed he was afeered to. Dat splains away de mystery.

De Freenerlogical Journal says dat in choosin' a wife we should be governed by her chin. A man am mighty apt ter be governed by de same thing after he's married.

Dar's two gauntlets what tests a man's bravery—marriage and deff. But after he has passed de fust one he don't mind der second.

Dar's more or less trouble in every family. Yer can't shet out dermestic troubles like yer can de wind or de rain or de sunshine, by stuffin' old hats and close in de windys.

Dis am a big kentry, but hit ain't half big ernuff for de man whose wife am chasin' him roun' de block wid a chair leg.

4238   4239

4241

4249

4248

4252   4253

26

Have fun with all your new boyfriends in Beloit!

Lois

37

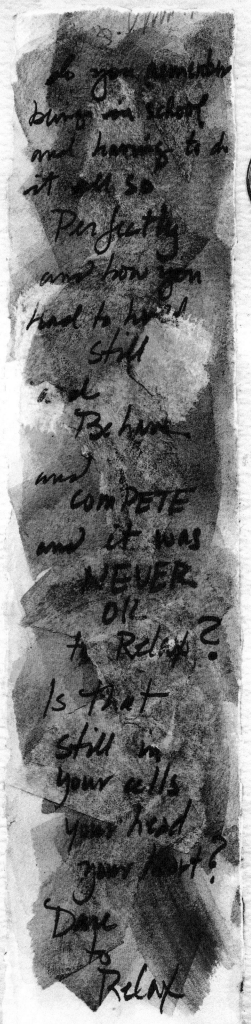

do you remember
bring in school
and having to do
it all so
Perfectly
and how you
had to hold
still
and
Be here
and
compete
and it was
NEVER
OK
to Relax?

Is that
still in
your cells
your head
your heart?

Dare
to Relax

38

Did You Know?
If your spoons, spinners and other bright metal lures get dull looking, vinegar and salt will brighten them. Rinse well.

THE MAD BULL;

OR,

LITTLE MARY'S ESCAPE.

———

I ALWAYS find that the more terrible and wonderful a story is the more thoroughly children seem to enjoy it. When I am commencing one sometimes I am not unfrequently stopped with a remark like this, "I hope it is very dreadful," or "Do let it be very sad." And I always find that if any of the terrors or wonders

Pickled Beets

2 cups sugar   1½ sticks cinnamon
2 cups vinegar   and (or)
2 cups water   1 doz. whole cloves

Simmer syrup about 5 minutes, pour over hot cooked beets (whole small beets or large beets, sliced) in hot, clean jars and seal. Makes enough syrup for about 4 pint jars of pickles.

Knives

This morning while doing the dishes
I thought of gypsies coming to my door
to sharpen knives.
My knives were sorely in need of attention
and since no gypsies were forthcoming
I carefully sharpened them myself,
thinking of whetstones.
My father had an ancient round whetstone
with a metal seat attached and a pedal,
you rode it like a gritty white pony.

He showed me how to sharpen a pocket knife
on a dark hand-held whetstone, spit on it,
carefully scrape the knife blade in a circle,
creating a dark wet place and
the edge of the blade
emerges shiny and sharp.

I thought I would like to be
an itinerant knife sharpener.
It would make me solid
and I could say "I'm a knife sharpener."

I would travel to people's houses
and sit wisely in their driveways
on my white whetstone steed
sharpening their knives,
offering bits of mysterious advice,
because having sharp knives
is strangely satisfying.
I would be the gypsy
come to my own door.

by rachel

To Roast a Turkey

TEN to fourteen pounds is a good weight for a turkey. If possible, select one that is dry-picked. Singe, wash thoroughly, cut off the head, dress, wipe clean again, but do not soak in water; stuff if desired, and truss or tie into shape. Brush entire surface with olive oil or melted butter, or cover breast and legs with thin slices of larding pork. Dust with pepper. Lay turkey on its back on a rack in a roasting pan. Barely cover bottom of pan with water; add a teaspoonful of salt. Place in a hot oven and let brown quickly on all sides, turning as necessary. Now reduce oven temperature, dust turkey with flour, and continue cooking, basting every fifteen minutes with water and fat in pan, until turkey is done—allowing fifteen to twenty minutes to the pound. A stuffed turkey requires a little longer cooking than one that is not. Cover breast during latter part of roasting, or keep it turned down in the pan. Serve with giblet or mushroom sauce.

March, 1897, has 31 days.

Woman Should be Natural.

A woman never loses anything by being real. For a woman to be natural is for her to be an object of respect and love. She was created to sway, not as men sway, by strong physical powers, but in her own way and by her more gentle qualities. A natural woman is the greatest power in the world today. By her very nature she conquers, whether she be the wife of an humble clerk or of a ten times millionaire.

"She is always so lovable, because she is so natural," was the graceful tribute I heard a group of women, a few evenings ago, pay to a young woman who had just left them.

"Men are so fond of her," said another woman in the group, "and yet no one would call her pretty."

Let artifice, sham or pretension enter into the nature of such a woman, and she would become at once an unwelcome guest where now she is bidden and eagerly sought for.

Some one may say, "Yes, the one you speak of is probably a rich woman, and she can afford to be lovable."

Not at all, my friend. She is the daughter of a man whose salary is too meagre for him to give his wife a servant, and this daughter helps the mother in her house work. She is the very sunshine of that home, simply because she never tries to appear what she is not.

Oval and round, are the
shapes of waiting; waiting
with the fullness
of potential. I can tell you
how I know this.
In my Kitchen I have jars
of seeds and beans —
pinto beans, cardamon pods,
lentils, sunflower seeds,
red rice, grains — and I'd
been admiring them when
I realized that they were
all oval, or round
quietly holding their potential
in a multitude of agreements,
each bean enjoying
its' individuality and its'
part in being joyfully
the same in the
collective
            by rachel ♡

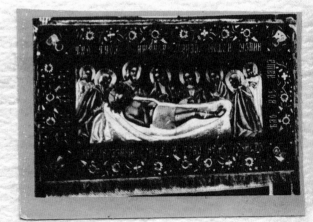

12. Do you like to work?
13. Do you like vegetables?

40

CLEOPATRA'S

MINESTRONE

BY RACHEL

SAUTÉ AN ONION IN
A LITTLE OLIVE OIL

ADD A CAN OF CHOPPED TOMATOES
3 OR 4 CUPS OF WATER
DICED CELERY
CHOPPED RED CHARD (ADD LAST)
CHOPPED GREEN ONIONS
1 CAN OF PIGEON PEAS
1\2 CUP KAMUT ORZO
1 CAN SOUP BEANS
(LENTILS · BARLEY · BEANS)

GARLIC POWDER
SALT
PEPPER
CAYENNE

Serve with Lemon

41

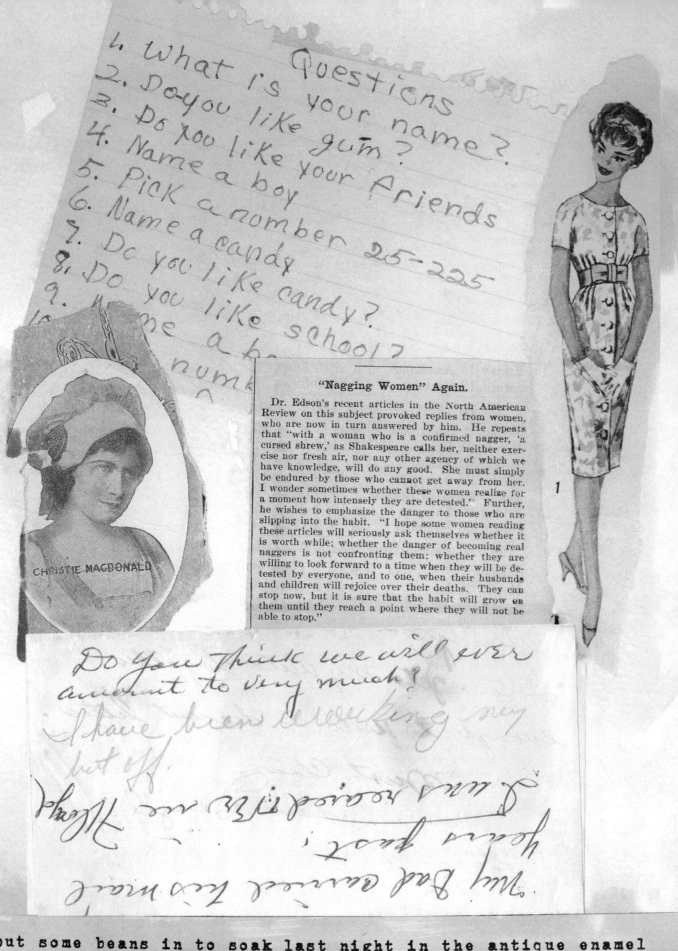

Questions

1. What is your name?
2. Do you like gum?
3. Do you like your friends
4. Name a boy
5. Pick a number 25-225
6. Name a candy
7. Do you like candy?
8. Do you like school?
9. ...

"Nagging Women" Again.

Dr. Edson's recent articles in the North American Review on this subject provoked replies from women, who are now in turn answered by him. He repeats that "with a woman who is a confirmed nagger, 'a cursed shrew,' as Shakespeare calls her, neither exercise nor fresh air, nor any other agency of which we have knowledge, will do any good. She must simply be endured by those who cannot get away from her. I wonder sometimes whether these women realize for a moment how intensely they are detested.' Further, he wishes to emphasize the danger to those who are slipping into the habit. "I hope some women reading these articles will seriously ask themselves whether it is worth while; whether the danger of becoming real naggers is not confronting them; whether they are willing to look forward to a time when they will be detested by everyone, and to one, when their husbands and children will rejoice over their deaths. They can stop now, but it is sure that the habit will grow on them until they reach a point where they will not be able to stop."

CHRISTIE MACDONALD

1

Do you think we will ever amount to very much?
I have been working my but off.

I put some beans in to soak last night in the antique enamel
blue pan and now am cooking beans. I love to use antique things,
especially in the kitchen! I feel very comforted that my cast
iron skillets will last my whole life!

Rachel

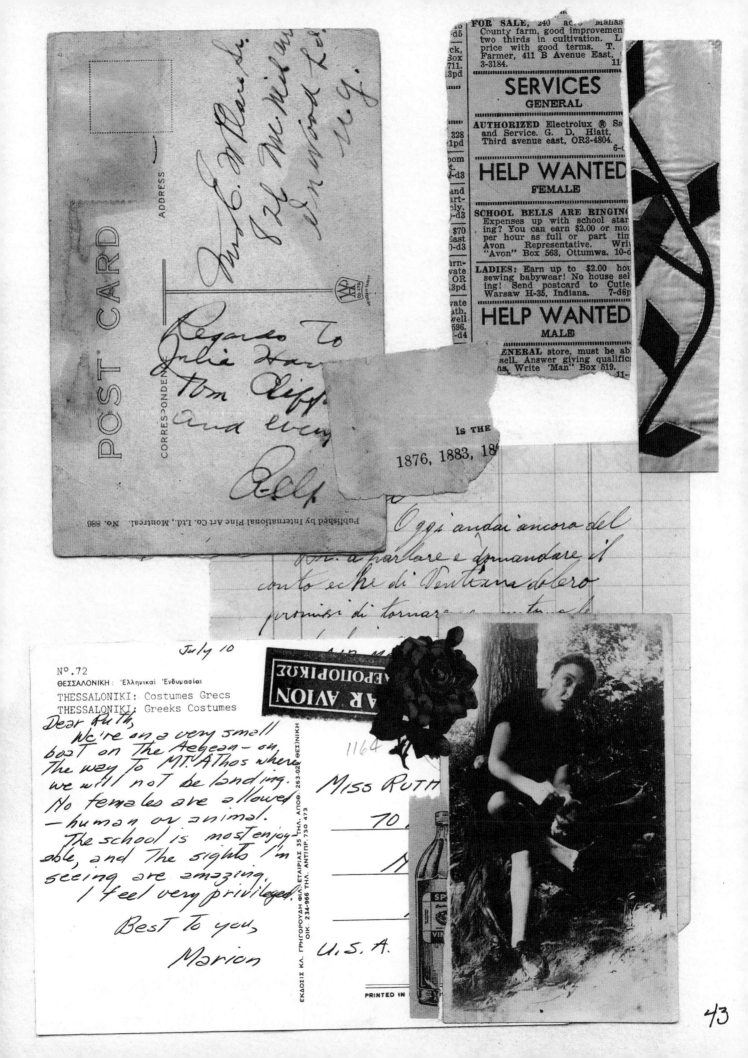

POST CARD

ADDRESS

CORRESPONDENCE

Published by International Fine Art Co. Ltd., Montreal. No. 886

Regards to
Julia Har...
Tom Cliff...
And every...
Ralph

Is the
1876, 1883, 18...

Oggi andai ancora del
...a parlare e domandare il
conto ecke di Ventana dolero
promisi di tornare ...

July 10

Nº.72
ΘΕΣΣΑΛΟΝΙΚΗ: Ἑλληνικαὶ Ἐνδυμασίαι
THESSALONIKI: Costumes Grecs
THESSALONIKI: Greeks Costumes

Dear Ruth,
    We're on a very small
boat on the Aegean — on
the way to Mt. Athos where
we will not be landing.
No females are allowed
— human or animal.
    The school is most enjoy-
able, and the sights I'm
seeing are amazing.
I feel very privileged.
    Best to you,
    Marion

AR AVION
ΑΕΡΟΠΟΡΙΚΩΣ

1164

MISS RUTH...

70...

U.S.A.

ΕΚΔΟΣΙΣ ΚΛ. ΓΡΗΓΟΡΟΥΔΗ ΦΙΛ. ΕΤΑΙΡΙΑΣ 35 ΤΗΛ. ΑΠΟΘ. 263-02 ΘΕΣ/ΝΙΚΗ
ΟΙΚ. 234-966 ΤΗΛ. ΑΝΤΙΠΡ. 730 473

PRINTED IN...

43

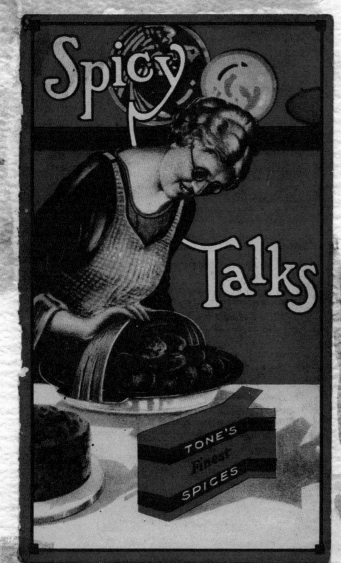

Spicy
Talks

TONE'S *Finest* SPICES

Would you cut meat this way?

NEW YORK, N. Y. (Æ)— "I was never used to being happy, so that wasn't something I ever took for granted."

The words came from a beautiful young woman— the brightest movie star of her generation, who, in the eyes of most Americans, had every reason to be happy. Her name was Marilyn Monroe. She was found dead Sunday.

Marilyn made the statement in an interview published in the current issue of Life magazine. Here, in her own words, are some of the late star's views on her life, her fame and her art:

"Sometimes wearing a scarf and a polo coat and no make-up and with a certain attitude of walking I go shopping—or just looking at people living."

IT IS NOT *SINFUL* TO BE COMMON——

BUT—

What woman wants to be the gossip of her friends simply because she served thin sliced bread for dinner, and entered the dining room last when dinner was announced by her maid?

Your Body
Smooth As Satin
Soft As Velvet

Corn Bread

2 cups corn meal
¼ teaspoon soda
2 teaspoons baking powder
1 teaspoon salt
2 beaten eggs
2 cups sour milk
2 tablespoons butter

Sift the dry ingredients together. Add eggs to milk, and stir into the dry ingredients. Add the melted butter. Pour into a hot greased pan about eight inches square, and bake at 425 degrees for 20 to 30 minutes.

44

I thought that you must re - sem - ble, A   Blue-beard fe - ro - cious, a-

In my kitchen
i bake bread
grain with tears
and oil
salt and memories
I wear green velvet
and an eyelet apron

an agony of remembering
flows down my arms
into the kneading
as i make bread
to nourish myself
I put it to rise
in the sunshine

to transform pain into
sustenance
i can tell it will be

a most beautiful bread
an alchemical loaf

one, that, perhaps,
only I
should eat.

____, 1929

mant and can be warmed and used. Your bread will keep moist longer if you use potato water for liquid, but bread made from milk has a softer crust and is whiter. During the process of making it, be sure you keep it in a warm place, not too hot or the bread will be coarse and dark in color. I will give you my recipe just as I made it and I do hope you have fine bread. If you should not, however, do not be discouraged for we all have to learn by experience.

2 tablespoons fat
2 tablespoons sugar
1 cake yeast
3 quarts flour
1 tablespoon salt
1 quart potato water
1 cup mashed potato

I have my yeast soaked in half a cup of warm water and then in the evening it is mixed with the other ingredients making a soft sponge. Let this rise over night in a warm place and in the morning add enough flour to make a stiff dough. Allow this to rise until double its bulk and then knead again. Make into loaves and when it rises again double its bulk, bake. Have the oven moderately hot for the first period, increase temperature for the second period, and then not so hot for thirty minutes more.

When the bread is baked, rub the crust with butter. I hope you have a rack to cool it on but if you haven't, remove the wire shelf from your stove, place it on two saucers and cool the bread on this.

I suppose you have made some New Year's resolutions and hope one of them is that you will write every week to your loving sister.—Leanna.

. Corn Bread

3/4 c flour
1 1/2 teas BP

1 teas salt

1/2 teas soda
1 1/2 c corn meal

1/4 c shortening

2 eggs

1 1/2 cups buttermilk

Sift flour and measure
Add bp salt and soda
Stir in corn meal and cut in shortn
as for pie crust. Add beaten eggs and
buttermilk and mix just enough to moisten
well
Bake in 8 in square pan 425deg for 30 m
min

Goddess Bread

This is a bread that combines
grains from many different
   cultures across time. When
you make it, think of the
women from Egypt, the Aztec women,
Incan, American, Middle Eastern,
women from the fertile crescent,
Scottish and Irish, African women,
and when you eat it, you will be communing
with all of them and this
will make your soul sing.

```
     Combine: 1 package yeast
              1/4 tsp ginger powder
              1 tbl sugar or honey
              2 tsp salt
              1 tbl oil
              4 1/2 cups warm water
              Stir gently and let the
              yeast bubble.
```

```
Meanwhile cook and cool: 1/2 cup pearl barley
                         1/2 cup wheat berries
```

```
Mix into the water yeast mixture:
              1/4 cup wheat germ
              1/4 cup ground flaxseed
              1/4 cup millet
              1/4 cup amaranth
              1/4 cup rolled oats
              1/4 cup cornmeal
              1/4 cup 7-grain cereal (hot cereal)
              1/4 cup sesame seeds
              1/4 cup quinoa
Add the cooked grains.
Stir in  wheat, white and spelt flours
to make a stiff dough and knead for ten minutes.
```

This is a sticky dough that requires patience but it
will behave and be beautiful and delicious. Sprinkle a
cast iron skillet with corn meal. Shape the dough into
small round loaves and bake in the skillet. And give
thanks to all the women who have gone before us.

by Rachel

Gilgamesh Goulash
— from the fertile crescent
by Enkidu Ballantine

Make one cup strong smokey tea

Add: 2 tablespoons pomegranite juice
  ½ to ¾ cup balsamic vinegar
  2 tsp olive oil
  salt
  pepper
  chopped garlic
  ½ cup cranberry juice
  dried parsley
  mint
  dash cayenne
  mix in bowl (a large one)

Chop up:
  15 green olives
  8 oz chicken
  1 oz pine nuts
  3 or 4 prunes
  roasted red pepper
  one onion
  one celery —
  broccoli
  scallions
  10 calamata olives

Soak — then chop & add
  5 dried shiitake mushrooms
  5 or 6 sundried tomatoes

Marinate all in the tea mixture. For a few hours then spread out in a large iron skillet and broil
  Serve on rice

It is tangy, smokey, filling, and incredibly delicious!

Rachel

Velma's Pickles

7lbs pickles putin salt brine 3 days

Brine strong enough to hold up an egg
Pour off and soak in clear cold water

for 3 days. Pour off and split your pickles
and put them into a weak vinegar water

with alum the size of a walnut for three

hours on back of the range. Stir with the
hand and do not let the water get too

hot. Pour off .
Now take

3 pints vinegar
3 pounds sugar
½ oz celry seed
½ oz whole allspice
½ oz cinnamon bark

Heat pickles in this and stir witha
spoon but do not boil. Have jars hot and

put in hot.

Pear Butter.
(two pints)

Two quarts peeled mashed pears, or pears put through food chopper.
One quart sugar.
One-half cup lemon juice.

Simmer pears and sugar a short time. Add lemon juice and cook until as thick as medium white sauce. Pour into sterilized jars and seal.

To make spiced pear butter, add one-fourth teaspoon cinnamon and one-eighth teaspoon cloves with lemon juice.

Saccharin Pickles
(Requested)

Here's my favorite pickle recipe. Try it and I'm sure it will be yours, too, it is so simple and sure to keep. Mix 3 quarts vinegar, 1 quart cold water, 1 scant cup of salt, 1¼ teaspoons of saccharin. Wash and pack cucumbers in jars, pour cold liquid over them and seal. Use spice to suit taste. This recipe will can 14 quarts. MRS. LEWIS YOUN_ Neosho, Mo.

Some people are nice
in the things they do
And some in the things they say,
But very few are quite like you--
Nice in every way!

49

Angel Delight Will Take High Honors
At Next Ladies' Bridge Luncheon

By Alvina Mattes
(The Register's Food Editor)

You might not sell this to the men, but it should please the ladies. It's an... delight, ...at

Turkish Lentil Soup

a cup of red lentils with 3-4 cups water. Boil until tender (10-25 min.). Put through food mill, add spoon of oil, a little tomato paste, lemon, red pepper salt and dried mint. To make thicker, add flour and water and reheat.

KR

Depressed while Frying Onions

I was depressed while frying
onions and sausage
building soup for a man I love
but pretend I don't
and trying to decide if I'd
invite him to eat it with me
or not
remembering to be mindful
while slicing and cooking
the grey onions
when the light through the prism
in the kitchen window
cast a marvelous and surprising
shard of a rainbow
across the skillet
turning the onions
red, orange, yellow
and I knew then it would
be a good soup
even if I eat it alone
but it would be better
if I shared it.
I can share my soup
much easier than
my heart.

by rachel

Thank You!

STRIKE MATCH ON BACK COVER

Buckwheat Cakes.

Take one pint buttermilk and one-quarter pint sweet milk; add a teaspoonful of salt, and stir in one pint of buckwheat flour; add one teaspoonful of soda and bake immediately, after beating well for a few minutes.

The Best Soup Ever - by rachel ♡

- Italian Jambalaya

<u>Sautee together:</u> (in non skillet)
- 2 strips smoked pepper maple bacon (diced)
- 2 mild Italian sausages (diced)
- diced mushrooms
- 1 clove diced garlic
- ½ chopped onion

Then transfer to soup pot after patting off fat
and <u>add</u>: water
- 2 stalks diced celery
- 2 diced carrots
- 1 can navy beans
- ½ cup brown rice
- ½ cup dried split peas
- ½ diced potato
- 1 bunch diced scallions
- 1 bay leaf
- salt and pepper
- cayenne pepper
- Simmer untill all is cooked
  an hour or two
- at the end, add 1 can
  drained smoked oysters

who is eating it
by <u>herself</u> because
she's <u>lonely</u> and her
boyfriend doesn't
even care at <u>all</u>
because he loves
<u>beer more</u>

Sumerian Goddess Soup
for Loved Ones
by rachel ♡

Sauté cubed beef and onions
and mushrooms in oil
Add: mushroom broth
    barley
    carrot
    celery
    scallions
    parsley
    salt
    pepper
    Smoky Hungarian Sweet Paprika

Simmer ~

Chop ingredients with attention and
love.
Stir with loving intent.
Serve with love in beautiful bowls.
Eat with careful attention
delight and gratitude.

52

Rachel Rose Salad

In an ancient Etruscan vessel:

4 cups Wild Rose Petals (pink and yellow)

1 cup Checkoslovakian rhinestones

1 whole snakeskin

2 wolf's teeth

2 teaspoons mercury

3 cups concentrated mystery

7 lion's whiskers

Two drops of blood

1 star ruby the size of a pigeon's egg

1 teacup of antique ink

Toss.

Christmas Ribbon Salad.

2 packages lime gelatin
1 package lemon gelatin
2 packages cherry gelatin
1 cup hot water
½ cup marshmallows
No. 2 can crushed pineapple
8-ounce package Philadelphia cream cheese
½ pint whipping cream

Prepare lime gelatin according to the package directions. Pour into a 15 by 10 by 2-inch pan and chill until almost set. Dissolve the lemon gelatin in the cup of hot water, add the marshmallows, which have been cut in small pieces, and stir until marshmallows are melted.

Add the cream cheese and 1 cup of juice drained from the pineapple. Beat with a rotary beater until blended. Then stir in one cup of the drained pineapple and set in refrigerator to cool slightly. Whip the cream and fold into the pineapple-gelatin mixture. Chill until almost thickened and pour over the lime gelatin.

Lastly, prepare cherry gelatin according to package directions and chill until the consistency of egg whites. Pour over the pineapple layer and chill until firm.

Always kept on hand in Mrs. Wiele's refrigerator are a pie crust mix and a sweet salad dressing. Three cups of the pie crust mix makes a double-crust pie, Mrs. Wiele said.

Kitchen Runes

Around the edges
of my wooden cutting board
is an ancient language
the runes of things
diced, things chopped
A thousand onions
speak out in the criss cross
hem of the board

The pie tin too it's
grey metal palimpsest
engraved with a sunburst
of runes of pies
the stories of eighty years
of sliced crusts told in the secret
language of knives

Who baked them?
What was her name?
What husbands were these pies
set before?

by rachel

54

Chalupas

Ory tortillas
until crisp

Spread with refried beans
(see ranch beans in this book)
that have been mashed

Add hot sauce.

half sliced tomato,

and top with grated cheese.

Put under broiler for a few
seconds to melt cheese, and serve.

Dorothy Price

<u>Tea and Toast</u>

Imagine your tea cup is three thousand years old,
it was made in Egypt by a High Priestess
during a magical ceremony
to bless and infuse every cup
of tea with celestial healing.

Imagine you had to scale
fifty foot cliffs for your honey
and carry it down on your back.

Imagine you dug the earth
and prayed and weeded
and danced and harvested
and chaffed and ground and kneaded
and baked the wheat for your bread.

Imagine you fed your beautiful
brown eyed cow nice grass
and you milked her and you churned
the cream and sang the Come Butter Come Song
and you paddled the butter into its mold
and this is the butter for your toast.

Imagine you walked to Tibet from here
and you gathered the tea in your skirt on a steep
windy hillside, and then you
dried the tea in the sun for days
watching over it, you slept beside it
at night under a full moon.

Imagine the Buddha made your teapot.
He gathered the clay by the banks of the Ganges
and fashioned a teapot just for you
and built a fire of sandalwood to fire it in, and he walked
to Nepal to get the turquoise he ground for the glaze for your
teapot and on it he painted a Lotus flower.

Imagine now, there are angels singing to you because
You are so loved, now, while you are having tea with cream,
and toast, with butter and honey.
Enjoy.

by rachel

Wash 6 large potatoes. Grate with skins, add one teaspoon salt, one or two pinches light pepper, two tablespoons flour, ¼ teaspoon baking powder and three eggs. Beat thoroughly, have pan hot, use vegetable or olive oil and put in pan using tablespoon making them as large or as small as desired. Enough here to serve 6 to 8 persons. Fry both sides to golden brown.

George C. Zulper,
Chicago, Ill.

(Mr. Zulper, we are glad that you wrote us about your particular way

May you ever be happy all your life.
make a good wife and get a good husband.

Ginger Bread. 1 teaspoon each
1/2 cup sugar   ginger
1/2 " shortening   cloves.
2 eggs   soda
1 cup Molasses   with sauce
2 1/2 cups flour   or
1/2 cup sour milk   whipped
1/2 teaspoon Cinnamon   cream

Thank You's and
Mom
Laura
Amy
Alan
Esther
Wayne
Terry
Jona
Anita
Jennifer
Rich
and everybody else who talked with me
Thank You!
Love
Rachel

Made in the USA
Charleston, SC
19 October 2013